The
Quotable
Ronald Reagan

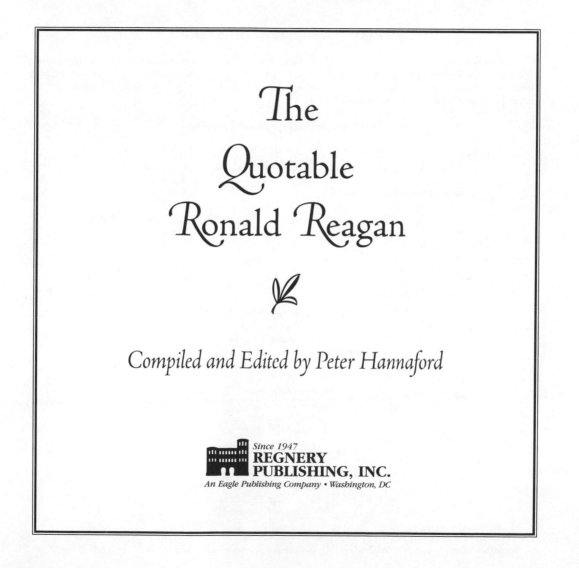

Compiled and Edited by Peter Hannaford

Since 1947
REGNERY PUBLISHING, INC.
An Eagle Publishing Company • Washington, DC

Library of Congress Cataloging-in-Publication Data

Reagan, Ronald.
    The quotable Ronald Reagan/compiled and edited by Peter Hannaford.
        p. cm.
    Includes bibliographical references.
    ISBN 0-89526-323-8 (acid-free paper)
    1. Reagan, Ronald—Quotations. 2. United States—Politics and government—1981–1989—Quotations, maxims, etc. I. Hannaford, Peter. II. Title.
E838.5.R432 1998b
973.927′092—dc21   98-43972
                                                      CIP

Published in the United States by
Regnery Publishing, Inc.
An Eagle Publishing Company
One Massachusetts Avenue, NW
Washington, DC 20001

Distributed to the trade by
National Book Network
4720-A Boston Way
Lanham, MD 20706

BOOK DESIGN BY MARJA WALKER

Printed on acid-free paper.
Manufactured in the United States of America

10 9 8 7 6 5 4 3 2 1

Books are available in quantity for promotional or premium use. Write to Director of Special Sales, Regnery Publishing, Inc., One Massachusetts Avenue, NW, Washington, DC 20001, for information on discounts and terms or call (202) 216-0600.

Also by Peter Hannaford

Recollections of Reagan: A Portrait of Ronald Reagan (editor)

My Heart Goes Home: A Hudson Valley Memoir (editor)

Remembering Reagan (coauthor)

Talking Back to the Media

The Reagans: A Political Portrait

Dedicated to my grandchildren,
Thomas and Patricia,
who will find here words of warmth, wit,
and wisdom to grow up by.

✒ Introduction

THIS BOOK HAD ITS BEGINNINGS in January 1993, although I did not realize it at the time. Early that month, right after the holidays, I received a call from Adam Meyerson, editor of *Policy Review* magazine. He asked if I had seen the quotations of Ronald Reagan in the new edition of *Bartlett's Familiar Quotations*. Although I had received a copy of the book for Christmas, I had not yet looked through it. I turned to it as soon as we rang off. There were three quotations, and footnote references to two others. It seemed clear to me that the person doing the selecting did not like the fortieth president of the United States. One quotation referred to uncontrolled government spending, another to people getting rich; a third was a seeming denial that anyone in the United States ever went hungry. The overall effect was to make Reagan seem superficial.

Absent were any of the words and phrases with which Ronald Reagan had inspired his fellow Americans. Gone was his pervasive optimism. Missing were his wit and humor in a meaningful context. The soaring words of his 1981 Notre Dame University speech, his "Reagan Doctrine" speech to the British Parliament (1982), and his tribute at Normandy to the soldiers of D-Day on the fortieth anniversary of their achievement (1985) were nowhere to be found.

As a writer I had been using *Bartlett's* for years and never considered it as having any bias. Rather, it seemed to me its mission was to collect memorable statements by famous and/or historically interesting people, without regard to their philosophical or political positions. Yet here was a case that seemed to belie that neutrality. Why, I wondered?

The answer was not long in coming. Justin Kaplan, general editor of *Bartlett's*, in an op-ed article in the *Wall Street Journal* on March 25, 1993, wrote, "I confess that I was less than dazzled by the Reagan presidency and its rhetoric." In the *Philadelphia Inquirer* he was quoted as saying, "I'm not going to dispute the fact that I despise Ronald Reagan." He is, of course, entitled to his opinion; however, if *Bartlett's* is to have credibility as a nonideological source for important quotations, its editor should have enough professionalism to keep those opinions to himself.

Perhaps the next edition of *Bartlett's* will correct this bias. Meanwhile, since 1993 I often found myself looking through the "Reagan shelf" in my study at the three or four narrowly circulated books of speeches and quotations from the beginnings of his presidency. Earlier this year, I decided it was time to collect the best of "The Great Communicator" over all the years of his public life. This book is the result.

That public life began with his October 1964 televised address, "A Time for Choosing," on behalf of Barry Goldwater's presidential candidacy—the speech that propelled Reagan onto the national political scene. It ended thirty years later, with his valedictory letter of November 1994, telling his fellow Americans that he had been diagnosed as having Alzheimer's disease.

In between you will find more than 330 quotations from his gubernatorial campaigns, his governorship, his 1976 and 1980 presidential campaigns, his 8-year presidency, and his post-presidential years until his retirement from public life. Several dozen subjects are covered, with a range of human emotions which may cause you to laugh or weep; to be inspired, reflective, proud of your nation, and wiser about human nature.

In cases where there is more than one quotation for a topic, they have been arranged in chronological order, from the oldest to the most recent. In these you will see the constancy of Ronald Reagan's convictions over the years, as well as the evolution of his rhetoric until, in his post-presidential years, it is quite reflective. In sum, the warmth, optimism, determination, and ability to inspire his fellow Americans are the qualities that stand out in the quotations of Ronald Reagan.

Peter Hannaford
Washington, D.C.
September 1998

✒ *Milestones in Ronald Reagan's Public Life*

OCTOBER 1964
"A Time for Choosing," nationally televised speech for Barry Goldwater

1966
Campaign for governor of California and election

JANUARY 1967 - JANUARY 1975
Governor of California (reelected in 1970)

1975 - 1979
Private citizen; campaign for the Republican
presidential nomination in 1976

1980
Campaign for president and election

JANUARY 1981 - JANUARY 1989
President of the United States (reelected in 1984)

1989 - 1994
Active as a former president

✹ Acknowledgments

OVER THE YEARS I HAVE REFERRED OFTEN to a small paperback book published by the late Joseph R. Holmes nearly a quarter-century ago. It's title: *The Quotable Ronald Reagan*. Joe conceived of and produced in 1973 and 1974 a weekly television program featuring Ronald Reagan in a question-and-answer session with a class of California high school seniors. The program was broadcast during school hours on the state's PBS stations. The only ground rule was: no discussion of politics, politicians, or the likely legislative fate of bills pending. Reagan and the students stuck to the rule. The program was popular and used as a teaching aid in history and civics courses at a time when public confidence in government institutions was low, in the wake of Watergate.

From this program, Joe got the idea of reprinting some of Reagan's most trenchant comments. Adding in quotations from a number of Reagan's speeches, he self-published the book. Joe went to the White House with President Reagan and worked there until his death in the early 1980s. In Joe's memory and to give continuity to his concept, I have adopted the title of his book.

My thanks also go to Carol A. Leadenham, assistant archivist at the Hoover Institution at Stanford University, and Lisa Vitt of the archival staff of the Ronald Reagan Presidential Library for their prompt and always cheerful responses to my requests and inquiries for dates, places, and texts. (Hoover houses the Reagan gubernatorial archive and his papers through the 1980 presidential election; the Reagan Presidential Library houses his papers from the presidential transition through his presidency and beyond, until his retirement from public life in November 1994.)

And, as with all my books, I give special thanks to my wife, Irene, who may be the most eagle-eyed manuscript proofreader in America. She can spot typos after I have read a page two or three times and thought it error-free. I thank her for this and for her constant inspiration and encouragement.

✒ Ability

We must never lose that sense of adventure,
that thirst for knowledge or that determination to explore
the outer limits of our own abilities.

— Remarks at the Citizens' University Committee dinner,
University of California at Riverside, May 18, 1973

🖋 Abortion

Simple morality dictates that unless and until someone can prove the unborn human is not alive, we must give it the benefit of the doubt and assume it is. And, thus, it should be entitled to life, liberty and the pursuit of happiness.

— *Alfred M. Landon Lecture Series on Public Issues, September 9, 1982*

✿ Affirmative Action

I am for affirmative action; I am against quotas. I have lived long enough to know a time in this country when quotas were used to discriminate, not end discrimination.

— *News conference, The White House, January 19, 1982*

✤ African-Americans

No other experience in American history runs quite parallel to the black experience. It has been one of great hardships, but also one of great heroism; of great adversity, but also great achievement.

— Address at the National Black Republican Council dinner, Washington, D.C., September 15, 1982

✒ Age

Age has its privileges, not least among them the opportunity to distill whatever wisdom comes from a long life of experiences.

— *Statement on the occasion of the 50th anniversary of D-Day, June 6, 1994*

✿ Agriculture

When government uses its coercive power to intervene in the free market place, agriculture can discover it has something worse to contend with than the corn borer or the boll weevil.

— *Remarks to the American Farm Bureau Federation,*
Los Angeles, December 11, 1972

✒ Alzheimer's Disease

I have recently been told that I am one of the millions of Americans who will be afflicted with Alzheimer's Disease.... I now begin the journey that will lead me into the sunset of my life. I know that for America there will always be a bright dawn ahead. Thank you, my friends. May God always bless you.

— *Letter to the American people, November 5, 1994*

✌ American Dream, The

The American dream that we have nursed for so long in this country, and lately neglected, is not that every man must be level with every other man. The American dream is that every man must be free to become whatever God intends he should become.

— *From the Reagan-Carter presidential debate, October 28, 1980*

American Spirit, The

We are the showcase of the future. And it is within our power to mold that future—this year and for decades to come. It can be as grand and as great as we make it.... No crisis is beyond the capacity of our people to solve; no challenge too great.

— Meet the Students, *taping for television, January 7, 1974*

I ask you to trust that American spirit which knows no ethnic, religious, social, political, regional or economic boundaries; the spirit that burned with zeal in the hearts of millions of immigrants from every corner of the earth who came here in search of freedom.

Some say that spirit no longer exists. But I have seen it—I have felt it—all across the land; in the big cities, the small towns and in rural America. The American spirit is there, ready to blaze into life if you and I are willing to do what has to be done; the practical things that will stimulate our economy, increase productivity and put America back to work.

— Speech accepting the Republican presidential nomination,
Detroit, July 17, 1980

American Values

I'm convinced that today the majority of Americans want what those first Americans wanted: A better life for themselves and their children; a minimum of government authority. Very simply, they want to be left alone in peace and safety to take care of the family by earning an honest dollar and putting away some savings. This may not sound too exciting, but there is something magnificent about it. On the farm, on the street corner, in the factory and in the kitchen, millions of us ask nothing more, but certainly nothing less than to live our own lives according to our values—at peace with ourselves, our neighbors and the world.

— Nationally televised address, July 6, 1976

✿ Anthem, National

I don't know all the national anthems of the world, but I do know this: The only anthem of those I do know that ends with a question is ours, and may it ever be thus. Does that banner still wave "o'er the land of the free and the home of the brave?" Yes it does, and we're going to see that it continues to wave over that kind of a country.

— *Remarks at the Republican Congressional "Salute to President Reagan" dinner,*
Washington, D.C., May 4, 1982

Appeasement

...*H*istory tells us that appeasement does not lead to peace. It invites an aggressor to test the will of a nation unprepared to meet that test. And... those who seemingly want peace the most, our young people, pay the heaviest price for our failure to maintain our strength.

— *Remarks to the National Guard Association of the United States,*
San Francisco, September 14, 1972

✒ Arms Control

Agreements on arms control and disarmament can be useful in reinforcing peace; but they're not magic. We should not confuse the signing of agreements with the solving of problems.

— *Address to the United Nations General Assembly,*
New York City, June 17, 1982

🖋 Assets

It is [another] fact of human nature: When a person owns assets—
a house, land, a small business or shares of stock in a big one—he or she
will look after those assets.

— *Address to the shipyard workers, Gdansk, Poland, September 15, 1990*

✒ Berlin Wall

Mr. Gorbachev, open this gate! Mr. Gorbachev, tear down this wall!

— Remarks at the Brandenburg Gate, Berlin, Germany, June 12, 1987

✒

It's been years since I stood at the Brandenburg Gate and called for the Wall to come down. It wasn't merely a polite suggestion. I was angry, because as I looked over the Wall into East Germany, I could see the people being kept away—their government didn't want them to hear what we were saying. But I think that they knew what we were saying and wanted a better life.

— Remarks upon being presented with a section of the Berlin Wall, Ronald Reagan Presidential Library, Simi Valley, California, April 12, 1990

✭ Bigotry

I know you have been horrified, as I have, by the resurgence of some hate groups preaching bigotry and prejudice. Use the mighty voice of your pulpits and the powerful standing of your churches to denounce and isolate these hate groups.… The commandment given us is clear and simple: "Thou shalt love thy neighbor as thyself."

— *Address to the National Association of Evangelicals,*
Orlando, Florida, March 8, 1983

❧ Brevity

As Henry VIII said to each of his wives, "I won't keep you long."

— *Opening remark to members of the American Business Conference,*
Washington, D.C., March 24, 1987

🖋 British-American Relations

Bismarck reflected that the supreme fact of the 19th century was that Great Britain and the United States shared the same language. And surely future historians will note that a supreme fact of this century was that Great Britain and the United States shared the same cause; the cause of human freedom.

> — *Remarks at the welcoming ceremony for*
> *British Prime Minister Margaret Thatcher,*
> *The White House, November 16, 1988*

❧ Budget, Balancing

Balance the budget by bringing to heel a federal establishment which has taken too much power from the states, too much liberty with the Constitution, and too much money from the people.

— Remarks at a rally for a proposed Constitutional amendment for a balanced federal budget, July 19, 1982

❧

Balancing the budget is a little like protecting your virtue: You just have to learn to say "no."

— Alfred M. Landon Lecture Series on Public Issues, Manhattan, Kansas, September 9, 1982

Budget, Federal

The size of the federal budget is not an appropriate barometer of social conscience or charitable concern.

— *Remarks to the National Alliance of Business, October 5, 1981*

✒ Bureaucrats

Government is too important to be left to those who are not too busy; the professionals who think government has some sort of divine right to tell people what is good for them.

— Speech to the American Dental Association,
San Francisco, October 28, 1972

✒

If a bureaucrat had been writing the Ten Commandments, a simple rock slab would not have had nearly enough room. Those simple rules would have read, "Thou Shalt Not—unless you feel strongly to the contrary, or for the following stated exceptions (See Paragraphs 1-10, Subsection A)."

— Address at the Marlborough School Graduation Ceremony,
Los Angeles, June 6, 1974

*E*very once in a while, somebody has to get the bureaucracy by the neck and shake it loose and say "stop doing what you're doing."

— *Remarks to students at Moscow State University,*
Moscow, May 31, 1988

✒ Business, Regulation of

I think that anyone who has a business has a right to run it the way he wants to. If he decides everybody has to wear a necktie or nobody has to, that is up to him. I just don't like to see government passing laws to do whatever government thinks he should do.

— Meet the Students, *taping for television, June 15, 1973*

✒

*W*e have all heard that if you build a better mousetrap, the world will beat a path to your door. Today, if you build a better mousetrap, the government comes along with a better mouse.

— *Speech in Cullman, Alabama, March 21, 1975*

✹ Californians

Californians are starters… but we are also stickers.

— Address to the California State Legislature,
Sacramento, May 6, 1991

✌ Campaign Trail, The

Once during the campaign some fellow said to me that he didn't think I was working very hard. He said, "You've got too good a tan." And I said, "Well, I've been doing a lot of outdoor rallies." And then he says, "Well, you talk too long then."

— *Remarks at a Republican Party rally, Reno, Nevada, October 7, 1982*

✍ Capital Punishment

I don't believe those who voted to reestablish capital punishment did so out of any feelings of vengeance or because they were bloodthirsty zealots. They simply believe that criminals who murder innocent women and children, who gun down police and engage in political assassination will not be deterred by anything less than the ultimate penalty—and they are right.

— *Remarks at the Sacramento Host Breakfast, September 7, 1973*

✒ Change

All great change in America begins at the dinner table.

— *Farewell Address to the Nation, The White House, January 11, 1989*

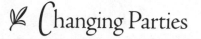 Changing Parties

I know what it's like to pull the Republican lever for the first time, because I used to be a Democrat myself and I can tell you it only hurts for a minute and then it feels just great.

— *Remarks at a campaign appearance, Bayonne, New Jersey, October 25, 1980*

❧ Character

... The character that takes command in moments of crucial choices has already been determined by a thousand other choices made earlier in seemingly unimportant moments. It has been determined by all the "little" choices of years past—by all those times when the voice of conscience was at war with the voice of temptation, [which was] whispering the lie that "it really doesn't matter." It has been determined by all the day-to-day decisions made when life seemed easy and crises seemed far away—the decision that, piece by piece, bit by bit, developed habits of discipline or of laziness; habits of self-sacrifice or self-indulgence; habits of duty and honor and integrity— or dishonor and shame.

— *Commencement address,*
The Citadel, South Carolina, May 15, 1993

THE QUOTABLE RONALD REAGAN

✹ Character Assassinations

*T*oo often character assassination has replaced debate in principle here in Washington. Destroy someone's reputation, and you don't have to talk about what he stands for.

> — *Remarks to the National Alliance of Business,*
> *Washington, D.C., September 14, 1987*

❧ China

...The future is hard to predict in China, although I am betting on the triumph there of the tidal wave of freedom that is sweeping the world.

— *From Ronald Reagan's memoir,* An American Life, *1990*

 Christmas

Meaning no disrespect to the religious convictions of others, I still can't help wondering how we can explain away what to me is the greatest miracle of all and which is recorded in history. No one denies there was such a man, that he lived and that he was put to death by crucifixion.

Where… is the miracle I spoke of? Well consider this and let your imagination translate the story into our own time—possibly to your own home town. A young man whose father is a carpenter grows up working in his father's shop. One day he puts down his tools and walks out of his father's shop. He starts preaching on street corners and in the nearby countryside, walking from place to place, preaching all the while, even though he is not an ordained minister. He never gets farther than an area perhaps 100 miles wide at the most.

He does this for three years. Then he is arrested, tried and convicted. There is no court of appeal, so he is executed at age 33 along with two common thieves. Those in charge of his execution roll dice to see who gets his clothing—the only possessions he has. His family cannot afford a burial place for him so he is interred in a borrowed tomb. End of story? No, this uneducated, propertyless young man who… left no written word has, for 2,000 years, had a greater effect on the world than all the rulers, kings, emperors; all the conquerors, generals and admirals; all the scholars, scientists and philosophers who have ever lived—all of them put together.

How do we explain that? …unless he really was what he said he was.

— Daily radio commentary (syndicated), December 1978

🖋 Churchill, Winston

His Fulton speech was a firebell in the night; a Paul Revere warning that tyranny was once more on the march.

— Address about Churchill's "Iron Curtain" speech, Westminster College, Fulton, Missouri, November 9, 1990

✒ Citizen-Politician

Although I held public office for a total of sixteen years, I also thought of myself as a citizen-politician, not a career one. Every now and then when I was in government, I would remind my associates that "When we start thinking of government as 'us' instead of 'them,' we've been here too long." By that I mean that elected officeholders need to retain a certain skepticism about the perfectibility of government.

— *Address to the Los Angeles Junior Chamber of Commerce, July 10, 1991*

🌿 Civil Rights

The battle against discrimination still goes on, and much remains to be done. But in a single generation, an entire nation recommitted itself to the cause of equal rights and used the full force of the law to ban, once and for all, racial bias in public education, in hiring and in the voting booth....

Nowhere does history offer a parallel to this vast undertaking. With all its flaws, America remains a unique achievement for human dignity on a scale unequaled anywhere in the world.

— *Address to the National Conference of Christians and Jews, March 23, 1982*

✒ College Days

The bonding which takes place in college is unlike any other experience. My young friends, savor these moments. Keep the memories close to your heart. Cherish your family and your friends. As I learned years ago, we never really know what the future will bring.

— Remarks at George Washington University,
Washington, D.C., March 28, 1991

 Communism

I believe that communism is another sad, bizarre chapter in human history whose last pages even now are being written.

> — *Address to the National Association of Evangelicals, Orlando, Florida, March 8, 1983*

*T*he principles of wealth-creation transcend time, people and place. Governments which deliberately subvert them by denouncing God, smothering faith, destroying freedom, and confiscating wealth have impoverished their people. Communism works only in Heaven, where they don't need it, and in Hell, where they've already got it.

> — *Remarks at the national conference of the National Federation of Independent Business, June 22, 1983*

*I'*m sorry that some of the chairs on the left seem to be uncomfortable.

> — *Address to the Assembly of the Republic of Portugal as some Communist members of Assembly walked out, Lisbon, May 9, 1985*

*C*ommunism was born in the ashes of feudal systems and was embraced, in its early days, by idealists and utopians, near and far. It died with the Berlin Wall, with the death of the Ceausescus, with the rise of Solidarity, with the Lithuanian declaration of independence and with other acts throughout what had once seemed an impregnable empire.

> — *Address to the Cambridge Union Society, Cambridge, England, December 5, 1990*

Compromise, The Art of

I have always figured that half a loaf is better than none, and I know that in the democratic process you're not going to always get everything you want.

— *Meeting with regional editors and broadcasters,*
The White House, February 9, 1983

✤ Congress

The Big Spenders in the Congress are at it again.... They've been inventing their miracle cures for which there are no known diseases.

— *Remarks to the Ohio Veterans' Organization,*
Columbus, October 4, 1982

✹ Conservatism

...Conservative thought is no longer over... on the right, it's the mainstream now.

— *Remarks at the Conservative Political Action Conference, Washington, D.C., March 1, 1985*

✒ Corporate Welfare

This is feeding the crocodile in the hope he will eat you last....

— Commenting on businesses clamoring for government subsidies, at a stop during his campaign for the Republican presidential nomination, February 1976

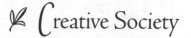 # Creative Society

...Let's adopt a creative approach and ask how we can use government to further free the people to allow us to reach our fullest potential.

> — *Television address in his first gubernatorial campaign, San Diego, California, February 1966*

The Creative Society... is simply a return to the people of the privilege of self-government, as well as a pledge for more efficient self-government—citizens of proven ability in their fields, serving where their experience qualifies them, proposing commonsense answers to California's problems, reviewing governmental structure itself and bringing it into line with the most advanced modern business practices.

> — *Gubernatorial campaign address at the University of Southern California, Los Angeles, April 19, 1966*

❧ Crime

*T*oday's hard liner on law and order is yesterday's liberal who was mugged last night.

> — *Remarks to the Citizens Committee for Law Enforcement Needs,*
> *Los Angeles, August 1, 1973*

❧

*O*ne legislator accused me of having a 19th century attitude on law and order. That is a totally false charge. I have an 18th century attitude. That is when the Founding Fathers made it clear that the safety of law-abiding citizens should be one of the government's primary concerns.

> — *Address to the Republican State Central Committee Convention,*
> *San Diego, September 7, 1973*

*I*t's time... that we acknowledge [that] the solution to the crime problem will not be found in the social worker's files, the psychiatrist's notes, or the bureaucrat's budgets. It's a problem of the human heart; and it's there we must look for the answer.

— *Address to the International Association of the Chiefs of Police, New Orleans, September 28, 1981*

✍ Critics

The finger-pointers and hand-wringers of today were the policy-makers of yesterday, and they gave us economic stagflation and double-digit inflation. There was only one thing fair about their policies: They didn't discriminate; they made everyone miserable.

— Remarks to the annual convention of the
Concrete and Aggregates Industries Association, Chicago, January 31, 1984

Deficits, Federal Budget

*A*t home, our enemy is no longer Red Coats, but red ink.

— Remarks on signing a presidential proclamation commemorating the 200th anniversary of the British surrender at Yorktown, Virginia, The White House, September 14, 1981

*L*et's be clear about where the deficit problem comes from. Contrary to the drumbeat we've been hearing for the last few months, the deficits we face are not rooted in defense spending. Taken as a percentage of the gross national product, our defense spending happens to be only about four-fifths what it was in 1970. Nor is the deficit, as some would have it, rooted in tax cuts. Even with our tax cuts, taxes as a fraction of gross national product remain about the same as they were in 1970. The fact is, our deficits come from the uncontrolled growth of the budget for domestic spending.

— State of the Union address, U.S. Capitol, January 25, 1983

... *T*he deficit doctors have their scalpels out all right, but they're not poised over the budget. That's as fat as ever and getting fatter. What they're ready to operate on is your wallet.

— Remarks at a meeting of the National Association of Home Builders,
Washington, D.C., May 16, 1983

$\mathcal{Y}$es, deficits are a problem. I've been saying so for more than a quarter of a century now. But the problem is not the size of the deficit, it's the size of government's claim on our economy.

— *Radio address to the nation, March 3, 1984*

$\mathcal{W}$e cannot reduce the deficit by raising taxes.

— *Remarks at the Conservative Political Action Conference, Washington, D.C., March 1, 1985*

✍ Destiny

You and I have a rendezvous with destiny. We can preserve for our children this, the last best hope of man on earth, or we can sentence them to take the first step into a thousand years of darkness. If we fail, at least let our children and our children's children say of us we justified our brief moment here. We did all that could be done.

— From "A Time for Choosing," address on behalf of Barry Goldwater's presidential candidacy, delivered on national television, October 27, 1964

🌿 Devolution of Power

We have found, in our country, that when people have the right to make decisions as close to home as possible, they usually make the right decisions.

— Address to the International Committee of the Supreme Soviet of the U.S.S.R., Moscow, September 17, 1990

✒ Dialogue

I've always believed that a lot of the troubles in the world would disappear if we were talking to each other instead of about each other.

— Remarks at the Ford Motor Company's
Claycomo assembly plant, April 11, 1984

✒ Diplomacy

... Diplomacy, of course, is a subtle and nuanced craft, so much so that it's said that when the most wily diplomat of the 19th century passed away, other diplomats asked, on reports of his death, "What do you suppose the old fox meant by that?"

— *Address to the 42nd session of the United Nations General Assembly, New York City, September 21, 1987*

✒ Distrust

Nations do not distrust each other because they are armed; they are armed because they distrust each other.

— *Remarks to students at Moscow State University,*
Moscow, May 31, 1988

✤ Diversity

We keep adding new Americans all the time… and the diversity of their backgrounds makes us all richer. I'll confess to getting a lump in my throat when I witnessed a swearing-in ceremony for new citizens. Written on their faces was happiness, pride and determination to pursue their vision of the American dream.

— *Address to the Los Angeles Junior Chamber of Commerce, July 10, 1991*

✑ Diversity, Managing

...There are 250 million of us [Americans] and we represent a dazzling range of interests. The process of dealing fairly with all of those interests takes constant management and adjustment at the local, state and federal levels.

— *Address to the Los Angeles Junior Chamber of Commerce, July 10, 1991*

✤ Divine Plan

I've always believed that we were, each of us, put here for a reason, that there is a plan, somehow a divine plan for all of us. I know now that whatever days are left to me belong to Him.

— Remarks at the annual National Prayer Breakfast,
Washington, D.C., February 4, 1982

✎ Drugs

The best hope for saving young people from drug addiction is education.

— *Speech to the American Dental Association, San Francisco, October 28, 1972*

✎

Hundreds of thousands of our young people have become hooked by narcotics, lured into tragedy and a life of shame by the Pied Pipers of the so-called drug culture.

Drugs are not a fad or a phase to be compared to flagpole sitting or goldfish swallowing. The use of hard narcotics is largely responsible for the increase in burglaries, muggings and many of the irrational violent crimes in recent years.

— *Remarks to the Greater Dallas Crime Commission, February 1, 1974*

The war against drugs is a war of individual battles, a crusade with many heroes, including America's young people and also someone very special to me. She has helped so many of our young people say "no" to drugs. Nancy, much credit belongs to you, and I want to express to you your husband's pride and your country's thanks. Surprised you, didn't I?

— *State of the Union address, U.S. Capitol, January 25, 1988*

 *Ecology*

---

*F*leas are part of the ecological cycle, but I doubt if a dog thinks he is doing something to destroy ecology by wearing a flea collar.

— *Remarks to the California Labor Federation, San Francisco, March 7, 1973*

✒ Economics, Zero-sum

The weakness in this country for too many years has been our insistence on… carving an ever-increasing number of slices from a shrinking economic pie. Our policies have concentrated on rationing scarcity rather than creating plenty. As a result, our economy has stagnated. But those days are ending.

— Remarks at the annual convention of the National League of Cities,
Los Angeles, November 29, 1982

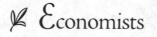 Economists

...One definition of an economist is somebody who sees something happen in practice and wonders if it will work in theory.

— Remarks to business leaders during a White House briefing on budget reform, March 13, 1987

❧ Economy, The

This Administration's objective will be a healthy, vigorous, growing economy.

— First Presidential Inaugural Address, U.S. Capitol, January 20, 1981

❧

This isn't a Keynesian Recovery produced by big-spending bureaucrats tinkering with aggregate demand.... Instead, this recovery was created by the incentives of tax-rate reductions, which shifted resources away from government back to American producers, savers and investors.

— On signing a Message to Congress, March 19, 1984

✿ Education

Our leaders must remember that education doesn't begin with some isolated bureaucrat in Washington. It doesn't even begin with state or local officials. Education begins in the home, where it is a parental right and responsibility.

— Remarks to the National Catholic Educational Association,
Chicago, April 15, 1982

✿

We're... proposing a voucher system to help parents of disadvantaged children. We want to give the states or individual school districts the option of using certain federal educational funds to create vouchers so that those parents can choose which school, private or public, they want their children to attend.

— Address to the National Catholic Educational Association, April 7, 1983

Secretary [of Education William] Bennett makes, I think, an interesting analogy. He says that if you serve a child a rotten hamburger in America, federal, state and local agencies will investigate you, summon you, close you down, whatever. But if you provide a child with a rotten education, nothing happens, except that you're likely to be given more money to do it with. Well, we've discovered that money alone isn't the answer.

— *Remarks to the National Governors' Association,*
Washington, D.C., February 22, 1988

THE QUOTABLE RONALD REAGAN

Education, Higher

The taxpayer is wrong who ignores the great increase in things we know—knowledge acquired since he was in school—and who demands "no newfangled courses. What was good enough then is good enough now." But, so is the student wrong who would eliminate all required courses and grades—who would make education a kind of four-year smorgasbord in which he would be the sole judge of how far and fast he ran in pursuit of knowledge.

— *Address to the California Federation of Republican Women,*
San Francisco, 1970

✒ Educator, The Role of the

[*T*he] educator is wrong who denies there are any absolutes—who sees no black and white or right and wrong, but just shades of gray in a world where discipline of any kind is an intolerable interference with the right of the individual.

— *Address to the California Federation of Republican Women,*
San Francisco, 1970

✿ Eisenhower, Dwight

In common with millions of his countrymen, Dwight Eisenhower fought not for territory, but for justice; not for plunder, but for righteousness. He fought for America's faith in the extraordinary qualities that lie within seemingly ordinary people.

— Remarks at the Eisenhower Library rededication,
Abilene, Kansas, July 27, 1990

Elders, Respect for

President Li comes from a nation whose people are known for their traditional respect for their elders. President Li, I can assure you that I'm doing my best to reestablish that tradition in our own country.

— *Toast at the state dinner for President Li Xiannian of China, The White House, July 23, 1985*

✒ Elderly, The

*I*t's been said that civilization is judged by how well it takes care of its young and old. I don't think that just means putting up money for the assistance of the old. There is a... lot more that the old need. They need to feel needed, for one thing.

— *Interview with* Government Executive *magazine,*
New York City, May 8, 1973

✴ Energy

The economic realities of the marketplace have done more to bring down the price of oil than all those years of frenetic government regulating.

— *Radio address to the nation, February 26, 1983*

❦ Entrepreneurs

We in government should learn to look at our country through the eyes of the entrepreneur, seeing possibilities where others see only problems.

— Radio address to the nation, January 26, 1985

❦

...Entrepreneurs and their small enterprises are responsible for almost all the economic growth in the United States.

— Remarks to students at Moscow State University,
Moscow, May 31, 1988

✒ Environment, The

*W*e do not have to choose between the environment and jobs. We can set a commonsense course between those who would cover the whole country with concrete in the name of progress, and those who think you should not build a house unless it looks like a bird's nest or a rabbit hole.

— Remarks to the Association of California Water Agencies, Sacramento, April 27, 1973

✒

*P*reservation of our environment is not a liberal or conservative challenge, it's common sense.

— State of the Union address, U.S. Capitol, January 25, 1984

✿ Equality

Recognizing the equality of all men and women, we are willing and able to lift the weak, cradle those who hurt, and nurture the bonds that tie us together as one nation under God.

— Address accepting the Republican presidential nomination,
Dallas, Texas, August 23, 1984

✒ Evil

Evil still stalks the planet. Its ideology may be nothing more than blood lust; no program more complex than economic plunder or military aggrandizement. But it is evil all the same. And wherever there are forces that would destroy the human spirit and diminish human potential, they must be recognized and they must be countered.

— *Remarks to the Oxford Union Society, Oxford, England, December 4, 1992*

🖋 Evil Empire

In your discussions of the nuclear freeze proposals, I urge you to beware the temptation of pride—the temptation of blithely declaring yourselves above it all and labeling both sides equally at fault, to ignore the facts of history and the aggressive impulses of an evil empire, to simply call the arms race a giant misunderstanding and thereby remove yourself from the struggle between right and wrong and good and evil.

— Address to the National Association of Evangelicals,
Orlando, Florida, March 8, 1983

❧ Fairness

Rebuilding prosperity… is the true meaning of fairness and compassion.

— Remarks at meeting with employees of the AccuRay Corporation,
Columbus, Ohio, October 4, 1982

❧ Families

Families stand at the center of society.

— *Remarks at a rally at the west front of the U.S. Capitol in support of a balanced federal budget amendment, July 19, 1982*

❧

When the liberals say "family," they mean, "Big Brother in Washington." When we say "family," we mean, "honor thy father and mother."

— *Remarks at a Republican Party rally, Waco, Texas, September 22, 1988*

 Farewell

May the road rise to meet you;
May the wind be always at your back;
May the sun shine warm upon your face,
The rains fall soft upon your fields,
And, until we meet again,
May God hold you in the palm of His hand.

— Old Irish prayer often quoted by Reagan

 Farmers

*F*armers are among the strong conservationists in this land. They earn their living from the land and they know man has to be careful with this precious resource.

— *Remarks to the Association of California Water Agencies, Sacramento, April 27, 1973*

…*O*n my way to the hall, a fellow recognized me and asked me what I was doing in Las Vegas…. I told him what I was here for, and he said, "What are a bunch of farmers doing in Las Vegas?" I couldn't resist. I said, "Buster, they're in a business that makes a Las Vegas crap table look like a guaranteed annual income!"

— *Remarks to state officers of the Future Farmers of America, Las Vegas, July 29, 1987*

Fate

I do not believe in a fate that will fall on us no matter what we do. I do believe in a fate that will fall on us if we do nothing.

— *First Presidential Inaugural Address, U.S. Capitol, January 20, 1981*

🌿 Federal-State Relationship

I have a dream that some day we can provide you with the revenue sources that have been co-opted by the federal government, so that local money no longer has to make the round trip through Washington before you can use it back in your local area—minus a certain carrying charge.

— Remarks at the annual meeting of the
National Association of Towns and Townships,
Washington, D.C., September 12, 1983

🌿

When our administration came to office, we took it as one of our chief aims to reawaken the federalist impulse and approach the Constitution with a new fidelity—in short, to restore the power to the states.

— Remarks to the National Conference of State Legislatures,
Washington, D.C., January 29, 1988

I can't help thinking that, while much of the 20th century saw the rise of the federal government, the 21st century will be the century of the states. I have always believed that America is strongest and freest and happiest when it is truest to the wisdom of its founders.

— *Remarks at the annual meeting of the National Governors' Association, Cincinnati, Ohio, August 8, 1988*

T here are a great many things that the state government should do that the federal government has no business doing.

— *Reagan, as quoted by Lamar Alexander in his* Little Plaid Book, *May 1998*

✒ Fitness

There is nothing as good for the insides of a man as the
outside of a horse.

— *Adage frequently quoted by Reagan*

🌿 Football

By now you must have gathered that I love football. It is the only sport in which men engage in bodily attack on each other. It's a kind of non-lethal war. You charge and fling yourself through the air to take down an opposing player before he can do the same to you. There is no other sport quite like it. It is total physical contact without hatred or death.

— Remarks at the University of Southern California - Notre Dame Luncheon, Los Angeles, November 23, 1990

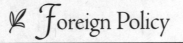 Foreign Policy

In 1980, the people made it clear they wanted a new direction in foreign affairs. Yet, changing America's foreign policy is a little like towing an iceberg. You can only pick up speed as the frozen attitudes and mistakes of the past melt away.

— *Address to the Veterans of Foreign Wars, New Orleans, August 15, 1983*

 Forests

$\mathcal{W}$e must cut trees no faster than trees are growing, to leave forests in such a way that, just as a farmer has another crop coming along, there will always be trees to cut and there will always be forests.

— *Remarks at a school in Rocklin, California, March 8, 1973*

✥ Freedom

Freedom is indivisible—there is no "s" on the end of it. You can erode freedom, diminish it, but you cannot divide it and choose to keep "some freedoms" while giving up others.

— Remarks to the National Broadcasting Company Affiliates, Los Angeles, May 4, 1972

✥

With freedom goes responsibility, a responsibility that can only be met by the individual.

— Remarks to a TWA Management Club dinner, San Francisco, May 2, 1974

*I*t is time to realize that profit, property and freedom are inseparable. You cannot have any one of them without the others.

> — *Remarks at a reception for Assemblyman William Bagley,*
> *San Francisco, October 15, 1974*

...*F*reedom is not the sole prerogative of a chosen few, but the universal right of all God's children.

> — *Address to the 40th Session of the United Nations General Assembly,*
> *New York City, October 25, 1985*

$\mathcal{F}$reedom is the right to question and change the established way of doing things.

— Address to the International Committee of the Supreme Soviet of the U.S.S.R.,
Moscow, September 17, 1990

$\mathcal{O}$nce people who have been deprived of basic freedom taste a little of it, they want all of it.

— Address to the Cambridge Union Society,
Cambridge, England, December 5, 1990

THE QUOTABLE RONALD REAGAN

🌿 Free Enterprise (Market Economy)

...America's prosperity was not a gift from the government or anyone else. Free enterprise, not government, is the source from which our blessings flow.

— *Remarks at the "Salute to the Reagan Years," Sacramento, December 12, 1974*

❧ Free Trade

Here in California, we are inescapably linked to markets around the globe. We want no barriers to ingenuity, no obstacles to our prosperity, for we know that truly free trade is fair trade—a good deal for Americans and a great source of jobs in the emerging economies of tomorrow.

> — *Remarks at the presentation of the Ronald Reagan Freedom Award to General Colin Powell, Ronald Reagan Presidential Library, Simi Valley, California, November 9, 1993*

🌿 Friends of America

Americans seek always to make friends of old antagonists.

— Remarks to students at Moscow State University,
Moscow, May 31, 1988

✤ Future, The

If you want to know which way to go in the future, you have to know which path you took in the past and where you stepped in a gopher hole along the way.

— *Remarks to the American Trucking Association,*
San Francisco, October 16, 1974

✤

America's best days lie ahead. You ain't seen nothing yet.

— *Remarks at a presidential campaign rally,*
Fairfield, Connecticut, October 26, 1984

Some may try and tell us that this is the end of an era. But what they overlook is that in America every day is a new beginning, and every sunset is merely the latest milestone on a voyage that never ends. For this is the land that has never become, but is always in the act of becoming. Emerson was right: America is the Land of Tomorrow.

— On accepting the Presidential Medal of Freedom,
The White House, January 13, 1993

 Gambling

I would hate to see legalized gambling in California, nor do I favor a lottery. We ought to finance the state by the strength of our people and not by their weaknesses.

— *Remarks at Boys' State, Sacramento, June 21, 1973*

❦ Generosity

Generosity is a reflection of what one does with his or her own resources and not what he or she advocates the government do with everyone's money.

— *Remarks to the Concrete & Aggregate Industries Association, Chicago, January 31, 1984*

🍃 Getting Credit

I have a little bronze plaque on my desk and I hope I can live by the inscription it bears: "You can accomplish much if you don't care who gets the credit."

— *Remarks at the Stanislaus Memorial Hospital's Appreciation Banquet,*
Modesto, California, June 27, 1972

✒ Giving

We make a living by what we get; we make a life by what we give.

— Remarks at the Herbert Hoover Library, West Branch, Iowa, August 8, 1992

 # Golden Rule

If we lived by the Golden Rule, there would be no need for other laws.

— *Remarks to the Sacramento Host Breakfast, September 7, 1973*

✒ Good Citizenship

Good citizenship and defending democracy means living up to the ideals and values that make this country great.

— *Remarks to Marine Corps basic training graduates,*
Parris Island, South Carolina, June 4, 1986

 Governing

---

*W*hen those who are governed do too little, those who govern can—and often will—do too much.

> — *Second Inaugural Address as Governor of California, Sacramento, January 4, 1971*

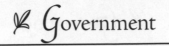 Government

In some dim beginning, man created the institution of government as a convenience for himself. And, ever since that time, government has been doing its best to become an inconvenience.

— *Remarks to U.S. Chamber of Commerce, September 24, 1972*

...Government is here to protect us from each other. Government cannot possibly set itself up to protect us from ourselves.

— *Meeting with editors and publishers, Los Angeles, February 13, 1973*

The… inescapable truth is: government does not have all the answers. In too many instances, government does not solve problems; it subsidizes them.

> *— Remarks to the U.S. League of Savings Associations,*
> *San Francisco, November 14, 1974*

…Government is the people's business, and every man, woman and child becomes a shareholder with the first penny of tax paid.

> *— Address to the New York City Partnership Association, January 14, 1982*

The best view of big government is in the rear view mirror
as you're driving away from it.

> — *Remarks at a meeting of Chief Executive Officers of National Organizations,*
> *March 24, 1982*

We have long since discovered that nothing lasts longer than a
temporary government program.

> — *Remarks at the Herbert Hoover Library, West Branch, Iowa, August 8, 1992*

... The nearest thing to eternal life we will ever see on this earth is a
government program.

> — *Often said by Reagan during his years in public office*

✹ Government Growth

Government has an inborn tendency to grow. And, left to itself, it will grow beyond the control of the people. Only constant complaint by the people will inhibit its growth.

— *Address to the Comstock Club, Sacramento, August 6, 1973*

✌ Government "Problem Solving"

When government decides to solve something, we have learned to be wary. The cure may not always be worse than the disease, but it is usually bigger and it costs more.

— *Remarks to the American Dental Association,*
San Francisco, October 29, 1972

*G*overnment does not produce revenue. It consumes it.

— *Remarks to the U.S. League of Savings Associations,*
San Francisco, November 14, 1974

🌿 Grants, Government

*A*ccepting a government grant with its accompanying rules is like marrying a girl and finding out her entire family is moving in with you before the honeymoon.

— *Remarks to the National Conference of State Legislatures, July 31, 1981*

🌿 Grenada, Invasion of

Grenada, we were told, was a friendly island paradise for tourists. Well, it wasn't. It was a Soviet-Cuban colony, being readied as a major military bastion to export terror and undermine democracy. We got there just in time.

— Address to the nation on the invasion of the Caribbean island nation of Grenada,
The Oval Office, October 27, 1983

✒ Gun Control

You won't get gun control by disarming law-abiding citizens. There's only one way to get real gun control: Disarm the thugs and the criminals, lock them up, and if you don't actually throw away the key, at least lose it for a long time.

— *Remarks at the "Salute to the President" dinner,*
Long Beach, California, June 30, 1983

✒

With the right to bear arms comes a great responsibility to use caution and common sense on handgun purchases. And it's just plain common sense that there be a waiting period to allow local law-enforcement officials to conduct background checks on those who wish to buy a handgun.

— *Remarks at George Washington University's Convocation,*
Washington, D.C., March 28, 1991

THE QUOTABLE RONALD REAGAN

✒ Heroes

Those who say that we're in a time when there are no heroes just don't know where to look. You can see heroes every day going in and out of factory gates. Others, a handful in number, produce enough food to feed all of us and then the world beyond. You meet heroes across a counter—and they're on both sides of that counter. There are entrepreneurs—with faith in themselves and faith in an idea— who create new jobs, new wealth and opportunity. They're individuals and families whose taxes support the government and whose voluntary gifts support church, charity, culture, art and education. Their patriotism is quiet but deep. Their values sustain our national life.

— *First Presidential Inaugural Address, U.S. Capitol, January 20, 1981*

Behind me is a memorial that symbolizes the Rangers' daggers that were thrust into the top of these cliffs. And before me are the men who put them there. These are the boys of Pointe du Hoc. These are the men who took the cliffs. These are the champions who helped free a continent. These are the heroes who helped end a war.

— Remarks at the 40th anniversary of D-Day,
Pointe du Hoc, Normandy, France, June 6, 1984

❧ Hispanics

*A*fter years of adversity and… discrimination, there is no doubt that Hispanics are taking their rightful place in American society.

> — *Remarks at a luncheon for representatives of the Hispanic community,*
> *The White House, September 16, 1981*

❧

*T*o every cynic who says the American dream is dead, I say: Come to the Hispanic business community; come see how entrepreneurs of Hispanic descent are not just building new corporations, they're building America's future for all of us.

> — *Address to the U.S. Hispanic Chamber of Commerce,*
> *Tampa, Florida, August 12, 1983*

✤ History

One of mankind's problems is that we keep repeating the same errors. For somewhere every generation, two-plus-two has added up to three, or in another place, five—four seems to elude some of us. This has happened in my generation, and I predict... it will happen to yours.

— *Address to the faculty and students of Eureka College at a library dedication, Eureka, Illinois, September 28, 1967*

✤

If I can leave the young people of Europe with one message, it is this: History is on the side of the free.

— *Address to the people of Western Europe from the Venice, Italy, economic summit, June 5, 1987*

*H*istory is no easy subject. Even in my day it wasn't, and we had so much less of it to learn then.

— *Remarks to winners of the Bicentennial of the Constitution Essay Competition,*
The White House, September 10, 1987

✒ Holocaust Victims

*H*ere lie people—Jews—whose death was inflicted for no reason other than their very existence. Their pain was borne only because of who they were and because of the God in their prayers.... For year after year, until that man [Hitler] and his evil were destroyed, hell yawned forth its awful contents. People were brought here for no other purpose but to suffer and die—to go unfed when hungry, uncared for when sick, tortured when the whim struck, and left to have misery consume them when all there was around them was misery.

— *Remarks at Bergen-Belsen Concentration Camp, Germany, May 5, 1985*

Human Life

If America is to remain what God in His wisdom intended for it to be—a refuge, a safe haven for those seeking human rights—then we must once again extend the most basic human right to the most vulnerable members of the human family. We must commit ourselves to a future in which the right to life for every human being—no matter how weak, no matter how small, no matter how defenseless—is protected by our laws and public policy.

— *Proclamation for National Sanctity-of-Human-Life Day, January 14, 1985*

✒ Human Nature

Despite the spread of democracy and capitalism, human nature has not changed. It is still an unpredictable mixture of good and evil.

— *Commencement address, The Citadel, South Carolina, May 15, 1993*

✍ Humor

I... used humor often with my friend Mikhail Gorbachev.... There were moments of frustration and disappointment, but there was always hope and our common ability to laugh.

— *Commencement address, Eureka College, Eureka, Illinois, May 9, 1992*

✒ Ideas, Source of

...Senator [Edward] Kennedy at a dinner recently, celebrating the 90th birthday of former Governor and Ambassador Averill Harriman, said that Averill's age was only half as old as Ronald Reagan's ideas. And, you know, he's absolutely right. The Constitution is almost 200 years old, and that's where I get my ideas.

— *Remarks at the "Salute to America" dinner, Houston, Texas, November 13, 1981*

✒ Impartiality

I know some of you are wondering if I'm going to say that line from that certain movie. But I know better than to take sides. So I've come up with what I hope will be a good compromise. As you may know, tomorrow I will flip a coin to officially start the game. So if you'll permit a little modification: Will you tell your teams to go out there and win one for the flipper?

— Remarks at the University of Southern California - Notre Dame Luncheon,
Los Angeles, November 23, 1990

✒ Indian Treaties

We've broken too many damn treaties. We're not going to flood them out.

— *Reagan commenting on his disapproval of the Dos Rios Dam project in California, which would have flooded Indian ranches and burial grounds. Quoted in Lou Cannon's coverage in the* Washington Post's *staff's book,* The Pursuit of the Presidency, *1980*

✒ Individual Initiative

Individual farmers, laborers, owners, traders and managers—they are the heart and soul of development. Trust them, because whenever they are allowed to create and build, wherever they are given a personal stake in deciding economic policies and benefiting from their success, then societies become more dynamic, prosperous, progressive and free.

— *Remarks at the International Meeting on Cooperation and Development,*
Cancun, Mexico, October 22, 1981

THE QUOTABLE RONALD REAGAN

✒ Industrial Policy (central planning)

Some believe that government planning is more efficient, so they rely on tax breaks and other subsidies to those businesses that already exist. But that never works... the most fertile and rapidly growing sector of any economy is that part that exists right now only as a dream in someone's head or an inspiration in his heart. No one can ever predict where the change will come from or foresee the industries of the future.

— *Address to the people of Western Europe from the Venice, Italy, economic summit, June 5, 1987*

✒ Inflation

When a business or an individual spends more than it makes, it goes bankrupt. When government does it, it sends you the bill. And when government does it for 40 years, the bill comes in two ways: higher taxes and inflation. Make no mistake about it, inflation is a tax and not by accident.

— *Remarks to the American Trucking Association,*
San Francisco, October 16, 1974

✒

Inflation is like radioactivity. It is cumulative. It piles up until one day you find it is out of control.

— *Remarks to the U.S. League of Savings Associations,*
San Francisco, November 14, 1974

*I*nflation was not some plague borne on the wind; it was a deliberate part of their [the Democrats'] official economic policy, needed, they said to maintain prosperity. They didn't tell us that with it would come the highest interest rates since the Civil War.

— Address accepting the Republican presidential nomination,
Dallas, Texas, August 23, 1984

✣ Injustice

When I say ours is the best and most advanced system of political freedom yet devised by man, I certainly do not mean we are perfect. I hope none of us will ever be so smug as to think there are no more injustices to correct, no more wrongs to right.

— *Remarks on Law Day at Mather Air Force Base, Sacramento, May 1, 1974*

🌿 Inner City Revival

*L*et the local entity, the city, declare this particular area—based on the percentage of people on welfare, unemployed and so forth—a development zone. Then, through tax incentives, induce the creation of businesses, providing jobs and opportunities in those areas.

— *Testimony before the U.S. Senate Finance Committee, 1972*

❧ International Relations

We can't build a safer world with honorable intentions and good will alone. Achieving the fundamental goals our nation seeks in world affairs—peace, human rights, economic progress, national independence and international stability—means supporting our friends and defending our interests.

— *Address to the American Legion, Seattle, Washington, August 23, 1983*

❧ Intolerance

...In the party of Lincoln there is no room for intolerance and not even a small corner for anti-Semitism or bigotry of any kind. Many people are welcome in our house, but not the bigots.

> — *Address accepting the Republican presidential nomination, Dallas, Texas, August 23, 1984*

❧

I consider it a tragedy that at some campuses in my own country, those who hold unfashionable ideas are hooted off the stage, or denied a forum in the first place. What a travesty of intellectual inquiry; what a perversion of the great chaotic, yet essential, marketplace of ideas that we call democracy. But then, I have always believed, at home and abroad, that the only cure for what ails democracy is more democracy.

> — *Remarks to the Oxford Union Society, Oxford, England, December 4, 1992*

✒ Iran-Contra Issue

... *I* take full responsibility for my own actions and for those of my administration. As angry as I may be about activities undertaken without my knowledge, I am still accountable for those activities. As disappointed as I may be in some who served me, I'm still the one who must answer to the American people for this behavior. And as personally distasteful as I find secret bank accounts and diverted funds—well, as the Navy would say, this happened on my watch.

— Address to the nation following receipt of the
Tower Commission's investigation report, The Oval Office, March 4, 1987

🌿 Irish Roots

I received a paper that told me that the clan to which we [he and Donald Regan, then Secretary of the Treasury] belong, those who said "Regan" and spelled it that way were the professional people and the educators, and only the common labors called it "Reagan." [Laughter] So, meet a common laborer.

— *Remarks to the citizens of Ballyporeen, Ireland, upon visit there, June 3, 1984*

✄ Isolationism

There is no way for America to turn inward and embrace isolationism in the world as it is today without jeopardizing all the progress we have made toward peace in this century.

— *Address to the World Affairs Council, Los Angeles, October 12, 1972*

✍ Israel

No people have fought longer, struggled harder, or sacrificed more than yours in order to survive, to grow and live in freedom.

— Remarks upon the visit of Israeli Prime Minister Menachem Begin,
The White House, September 9, 1981

🌿 Israel and Palestinians

I call on the Palestinian people to recognize that their own political aspirations are inextricably bound to [the] recognition of Israel's right to a secure future.

— *Address to the nation, September 1, 1982*

❧ Justice, American System of

Each new generation of Americans inherits as a birthright the legal protections secured, protected and expanded by the vigilance of preceding generations. These rights—freedom of speech, trial by jury, personal liberty, a representative and limited government, and equal protection of the laws, to name but a few—give every citizen a vested interest in American justice.

— *Proclamation for Law Day USA, April 15, 1983*

⚘ Justice, Criminal

Our commitment to criminal justice goes far deeper than our desire to punish the guilty or to deter those considering a lawless course…. Those principles will lose their meaning, and our citizens will lose faith in them if we concentrate solely on punishing criminals and ignore the suffering of those upon whom the criminals prey.

— *Executive Order 12360, creating the President's Task Force on Victims of Crime,*
The White House, April 23, 1982

⚘

The scales of criminal justice are still tilted toward protecting the rights of criminals…. Lenient judges are only lenient on crooks; they're very hard on society.

— *Remarks at the National League of Cities meeting,*
Washington, D.C., March 5, 1984

THE QUOTABLE RONALD REAGAN

✹ King, Dr. Martin Luther, Jr.

Martin Luther King, Jr., burned with the gospel of freedom, and that flame in his heart lit the way for millions. What he accomplished—not just for black Americans, but for all Americans—[is that] he lifted a burden from this country. As surely as black Americans were scarred by the yoke of slavery, America was scarred by injustice. Many Americans didn't fully realize how heavy America's burden was until it was lifted. Dr. King did that for us, all of us.

> — *Remarks on the anniversary of Dr. King's birth,*
> *The White House, January 15, 1983*

❧ Knowledge Revolution, The

*L*ike a chrysalis, we're emerging from the economy of the Industrial Revolution—an economy confined to the earth's physical resources—into [one] in which there are no bounds on the human imagination, and the freedom to create is the most precious natural resource.

— Remarks to students of Moscow State University,
Moscow, May 31, 1988

✌ Labor

... When I was young, golf was a sissy, rich man's game. So were boating and skiing and horseback riding. Today, they're weekend sports for the working man; he doesn't have to go to Labor Day picnics.

— *Remarks to a group of middle-aged labor leaders, California, Labor Day, 1970*

✌

Let me make our goal... very clear: jobs, jobs, jobs and more jobs.... Our policy has been and will continue to be: What is good for the American workers is good for America.

— *The President's Labor Day Message, September 4, 1981*

✒ Land-Use Planning

Land-use planning is so intricately bound up with the question of basic property rights that the only proper place to deal with it is at the state level. A land-use plan which works well in one state may not in another. Surely, it should be for the individual state to decide, and not rest in the hands of a bureaucrat or social engineer in Washington.

> — Press conference opening statement, National Governors' Conference,
> Seattle, Washington, June 1974

🖋 Las Vegas

Las Vegas is really a wonderful place. Where else outside of government do people throw money away? The big difference, of course, is that here you can do it yourself; in government, we do it for you.

— Remarks to the National Sheriff's Association,
Las Vegas, Nevada, June 19, 1967

✒ Law, Respect for

The teaching of respect for the law cannot be left to education alone. It is a responsibility we all must assume, in our daily lives, in every school, in our churches, throughout our social structure.

— *Remarks to a TWA Management Club dinner, San Francisco, May 2, 1974*

🌿 Leader, The Life of a

...*L*ife at the top is frequently a lonely business.

> — *Address to the Cambridge Union Society,*
> *Cambridge, England, December 5, 1990*

✒ Leadership

A leader, once convinced [that] a particular course of action is the right one, must have the determination to stick with it and be undaunted when the going gets rough.

— *Address to the Cambridge Union Society,*
Cambridge, England, December 5, 1990

THE QUOTABLE RONALD REAGAN

✒ Legacy

… **W**hatever else history may say about me when I'm gone, I hope it will record that I appealed to your best hopes, not your worst fears; to your confidence rather than your doubts. My dream is that you will travel the road ahead with liberty's lamp guiding your steps and opportunity's arm steadying your way.

> — *Address to the Republican National Convention,*
> *Houston, Texas, August 17, 1992*

✿ Legislating

*I*f you like laws and sausages, you should never watch either one being made.

— *Quoting Germany's 19th century "Iron Chancellor" Otto von Bismarck at a campaign stop, Oklahoma City, June 4, 1976*

✒ Liberalism

It has nothing more to say, nothing to add to the debate. It has spent its intellectual capital, such as it was—and it has done its deeds.

— *Remarks at the Conservative Political Action Conference, Washington, D.C., March 1, 1985*

✒ Liberty

---

*I*ndividual liberty depends upon keeping government under control.

— *Interview with Radio News West, Los Angeles, December 30, 1974*

✒ Love

...*L*ove is never wasted; love is never lost. Love lives on and sees us through sorrow. From the moment love is born, it is always with us, keeping us aloft in the time of flooding and strong in the time of trial.

— *Remarks at the memorial service for members of the Army's 101st Airborne Division, killed in an airplane crash, Fort Campbell, Kentucky, December 16, 1985*

✤ Management Style

The best you can do is try to get the best advice you can, listen carefully to many different views, make your decision and implement it with care, and keep testing your judgment to see if you need to make adjustments.

— *Interview with* Le Figaro, *December 22, 1983*

✱ Maturity

$\mathcal{M}$aturity is a matter of becoming comfortable with yourself with the world around you as time moves on and circumstances change.

— *Commencement address, Eureka College, Eureka, Illinois, May 9, 1982*

Medal of Freedom

From time to time I have been called the Great Communicator. But I'll tell you, it's no easy thing to communicate what I feel right now.

> — On receiving the Presidential Medal of Freedom,
> The White House, January 13, 1993

❦ Middle East

Let us remember that whether we be Christian or Jew or Moslem, we are all children of Abraham, we are all children of the same God.

— *Remarks upon the visit of Israeli Prime Minister Menachem Begin,*
The White House, September 9, 1981

✐ Monopoly

A great many people today who call themselves liberals are not against monopoly if it is a government or labor monopoly. Well, I think monopoly is wrong, not just who is doing it.

— Meet the Students, *taping for television, Sacramento, September 17, 1973*

✒ Mothers

To our mothers we owe our highest esteem, for it is from their gift of life that the flow of events begins that shapes our destiny. A mother's love, nurturing and beliefs are among the strongest influences molding the development and character of our youngsters. As Henry Ward Beecher wrote, "What a mother sings to the cradle goes all the way down to the coffin."

— *Proclamation for Mother's Day, April 6, 1983*

I find my thoughts turning to my own mother, Nelle Reagan. She was a truly remarkable woman—ever so strong in her determination, yet always tender, always giving of herself to others. She never found time in her life to complain; she was too busy living those values she sought to impart in my brother and myself. She was the greatest influence on my life, and as I think of her this weekend I remember the words of Lincoln, "All that I am, or hope to be, I owe to my mother."

— *Radio address to the nation, Mother's Day, May 11, 1985*

✒ Mother Teresa

... This is the first time I've given the Medal of Freedom with the intuition that the recipient might take it home, melt it down and turn it into something that can be sold to help the poor.

— On presenting the Presidential Medal of Freedom to Mother Teresa,
The White House, June 20, 1985

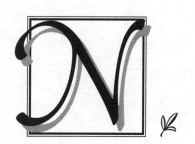

✒ Nafta

...Nafta [North American Free Trade Agreement] is unique and new: It offers a combination of economic growth, opportunity, benefits to workers and environmental sensitivity never before seen in the world.

— Remarks to the North American Forum,
Ronald Reagan Presidential Library, September 11, 1992

❧ National Debt, The

We don't have a trillion-dollar debt because we haven't taxed enough; we have a trillion-dollar debt because we spend too much.

— *Remarks to the National Association of Realtors, March 28, 1982*

❧

When I was in the fifth grade, I'm not sure I knew what a national debt was. Of course, when I was in the fifth grade, we didn't have one.

— *Remarks at a luncheon for members of the President's Advisory Council on Private Sector Initiatives, The White House, June 28, 1983*

❧ National Defense

A truly successful army is one that, because of its strength and ability and dedication, will not be called upon to fight, for no one will dare to provoke it.

— *Address at the United States Military Academy,*
West Point, New York, May 27, 1981

❧

The top priority of the federal government is the safety of this country.

— *Address to a joint session of the Oklahoma State Legislature,*
March 16, 1982

When we've taken up arms, it has been for the defense of freedom for ourselves and for other peaceful nations who needed our help. But now, faced with the development of weapons of immense destructive power, we have no choice but to maintain ready defense forces that are second to none. Yes, the cost is high, but the price of neglect would be infinitely higher.

— *Remarks at the recommissioning of the USS New Jersey,*
Long Beach, California, December 28, 1982

*I*t is always very easy and very tempting politically to come up with arguments for neglecting defense spending in time of peace. One of the great tragedies of this century was that it was only after... a ruthless adversary, Adolf Hitler, deliberately weighed the risks and decided to strike that the importance of a strong defense was realized too late. That was what happened in the years leading up to World War II. And... it's a mistake that America and the free world must never make again.

— *Radio address to the nation, February 19, 1983*

✒ NATO

NATO [North Atlantic Treaty Organization] will soon begin its fifth decade. The North Atlantic alliance is the most successful in history. While other alliances have been formed to win wars, our fundamental purpose is to prevent war while preserving and extending the frontiers of freedom.

— Remarks to reporters following the NATO "summit" meeting in Brussels, Belgium, March 3, 1988

 Negotiating

Before I took up my current line of work, I got to know a thing or two about negotiating when I represented the Screen Actors Guild in contract talks with the studios. After the studios, Gorbachev was a snap.

— Remarks to the National Chamber Foundation,
Washington, D.C., November 17, 1988

✒ Nuts

California produces 40 percent of America's fresh fruits, vegetables and nuts—the kind you eat. We have had a bumper crop of the other variety, too… the kind who would have us turn back the clock, forget about developing and maintaining the water supply we need for crops, for people and for industries.

— Remarks to the Association of California Water Agencies,
Sacramento, April 27, 1973

✒ On Being Shot

(remarks after John Hinckley's attempted assassination of him, March 30, 1981)

Honey, I forgot to duck!

> — *To his wife, Nancy, March 30, 1981*

✒

I hope you guys are all Republicans.

> — *To the surgeons about to operate on him, March 30, 1981*

✒

You mean this may happen several times more?

> — *To a nurse at George Washington University Hospital who told him, "Keep up the good work," March 31, 1981*

Ruined one of my best suits.

— *To his daughter Maureen, March 31, 1981*

After all the time I spent with G.W. doctors, it seems fitting that I now become one!

— *Remarks at George Washington University's Convocation, on receiving an honorary doctorate, March 28, 1991*

✒ One Nation

In recent years there have been voices raised… that would so emphasize our heritage—where we came from—they would separate us once again and have a nation of separatist groups based on ethnic, racial and religious lines. Don't let that happen.

— *Remarks at Boys' State, Sacramento, June 21, 1973*

✒ O'Neill, Tip

I think the fact of our friendship is testimony to the political system that we're part of, and the country we live in; a country which permits two not-so-shy and not-so-retiring Irishmen to have it out on the issues, rather than on each other or their countrymen.

— *Remarks at a dinner honoring Speaker of the House of Representatives Thomas P. ("Tip") O'Neill, Washington, March 17, 1986*

✒ Optimism

The history of our civilization, the great advances that made it possible, is not a story of cynics or doom criers. It is a gallant chronicle of the optimists, the determined people, men and women, who dreamed great dreams and dared to try whatever it took to make them come true.

— *Remarks at the Dedication of the California State Water Project's Perris Dam,*
Riverside, May 18, 1973

I... have been described as an undying optimist, always seeing a glass half full when some see it as half empty. And, yes, it's true—I always see the sunny side of life. And that's not just because I've been blessed by achieving so many of my dreams. My optimism comes not just from my strong faith in God, but from my strong and enduring faith in man.

— *Remarks at the dedication of the Ronald Reagan Presidential Library, Simi Valley, California, November 4, 1991*

✹ *Origins*

*I*n this dynamic world, it doesn't matter where you came from. It's where you're going that really counts.

> — *Remarks to the North American Forum,*
> *Ronald Reagan Presidential Library, September 11, 1992*

✒ Overconfidence

President Dewey warned me not to get overconfident.

— *Statement prior to announcing his candidacy for*
Governor of California in 1966

❧ Parents of Ronald Reagan

He [father, Jack Reagan] was the best storyteller I've ever heard and the strongest man of principle I've ever known. He believed in honesty and hard work.

In the darkest days of the Depression, when they [Jack and Nelle Reagan] themselves could barely scrape by, no one ever came to their door in need of a meal who Nelle sent away empty-handed.

So, now we come to the end of this last campaign, and I just hope Nelle and Jack are looking down on us right now and nodding their heads and saying their kid did them proud.

— *Remarks at a presidential campaign rally for Vice President George Bush,*
San Diego, November 7, 1988

✤ Patriotism

An informed patriotism is what we want.

— *Farewell Address to the Nation, The White House, January 11, 1989*

✶ Peace

The dustbin of history is littered with the remains of those countries that relied on diplomacy to secure their freedom. We must never forget... in the final analysis... that it is our military, industrial and economic strength that offers the best guarantee of peace for America in times of danger.

— *Remarks at a reception for congressional candidate Clifford Carlson, Chicago, September 10, 1974*

✶

As for the enemies of freedom, those who are potential adversaries, they will be reminded that peace is the highest aspiration of the American people. We will negotiate for it, sacrifice for it; we will never surrender for it, now or ever.

— *First Presidential Inaugural Address, U.S. Capitol, January 20, 1981*

$\mathcal{P}$eace is not the absence of conflict, but the ability to cope with conflict by peaceful means.

— *Commencement address, Eureka College, Eureka, Illinois, May 9, 1982*

Poise

I have learned that one of the most important rules in politics is poise—which means looking like an owl after you have behaved like a jackass.

— *Legislative luncheon, Governor's Office, Sacramento, August 9, 1973*

✒ Political Experience

_I_ don't know of anybody who was born holding public office. I am not a professional politician. The man who currently has the job has more political experience than anybody [else]. That's why I'm running.

— _Remarks at a campaign stop during the 1966 campaign_
for Governor of California

✒ Politicians

Let me tell you what I have learned from looking at those elected to office from the inside. For every one that's bad, for every one that can be bought, I will tell you there are scores who have never done a favor on the basis of someone's help in getting them elected or on the basis of a campaign contribution.

— Remarks at Boys' State, Sacramento, June 21, 1973

✒

The people who hold public office today are no better, no worse than the people that send them to public office, and you cannot expect them to be. They are representative of you.

— Remarks at Boys' State, Sacramento, June 21, 1973

*O*ne thing our Founding Fathers could not foresee... was a nation governed by professional politicians who had a vested interest in getting reelected. They probably envisioned a fellow serving a couple of hitches and then looking... forward to getting back to the farm.

— Meet the Students, *taping for television, Sacramento, September 17, 1973*

🌿 Politics

Politics is supposed to be the second-oldest profession. I have come to realize that it bears a very close resemblance to the first.

— *Remarks at a business conference, Los Angeles, March 2, 1977*

❧ Pollution

---

*W*e have tried to apply common sense to our pollution problems....
There are three kinds of pollution today: real, hysterical and political.

— Remarks to the Association of California Water Agencies,
Sacramento, April 27, 1973

🖋 Population

$\mathcal{Y}$ou could take the entire population of the United States and put it into the land area of only two states—California and Texas—and you would still have a population density lower than that of most of Western Europe.

— Remarks to the Association of California Water Agencies,
Sacramento, April 27, 1973

✌ Pornography

Just as we assume a responsibility to guard our young people up to a certain age from the possible harmful effects of alcohol and tobacco, so do I believe we have a... responsibility to protect them from the... harmful effects of exposure to smut and pornography.

— *First Inaugural Address as Governor of California,*
Sacramento, January 2, 1967

✹ Prayer

The Constitution was never meant to prevent people from praying; its declared purpose was to protect their freedom to pray.

— Radio address to the nation, September 18, 1982

✹

Unfortunately, in the last two decades we've experienced an onslaught of such twisted logic that if Alice were visiting America, she might think she'd never left Wonderland. We're told that it somehow violates the rights of others to permit students in school who desire to pray to do so.... We can and must respect the rights of those who are non-believers, but we must not cut ourselves off from this indispensable source of strength and guidance.

— Remarks at a School Prayer Day candle-lighting ceremony,
Washington, D.C., September 25, 1982

✒ Preparedness

We will always remember. We will always be proud. We will always be prepared, so we may always be free.

— *Remarks commemorating the 40th anniversary of D-Day, overlooking Omaha Beach, Normandy, France, June 6, 1984*

President's Responsibility

It is the responsibility of the President of the United States... to ensure that the safety of our people cannot be successfully threatened by a hostile foreign power.

— Speech accepting the Republican presidential nomination,
Detroit, July 17, 1980

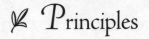 Principles

---

Presidents come and go. History comes and goes, but principles endure....

— *On receiving the Presidential Medal of Freedom,*
The White House, January 13, 1993

✒ Private Sector

...We have to realize that this country in its private sector has been fighting the most successful war on poverty the world has seen for the last 200 years.

— *Address to the Merchants & Manufacturers Association, Los Angeles, 1968*

❧ Profit

Profit is the legitimate earnings that someone gets on his investment. The average citizen should understand it if he has a savings account. The bank pays him for the privilege of using his money.

— *Remarks at a reception for a legislator, Palo Alto, California, February 7, 1974*

✒ Progress

$\mathcal{W}$e believed then and now: There are no limits to growth and human progress when men and women are free to follow their dreams. And we were right to believe that. Tax rates have been reduced, inflation cut dramatically and more people are employed than ever before in our history.

— *Second Presidential Inaugural Address, U.S. Capitol, January 20, 1985*

✒ Prosperity

In the long post-World War II years of affluence, perhaps we have forgotten that no one gave America the world's highest standard of living. We earned it, by being the most productive and efficient industrial nation in the world.

— *Remarks to the Lincoln Club of Los Angeles, February 14, 1972*

✒

We must prolong and protect our growing prosperity so it doesn't become just a passing phase, a natural adjustment between periods of recession. We must move further to provide incentive and make America the investment capital of the world.

— *Remarks at the Conservative Political Action Conference,*
Washington, D.C., March 1, 1985

THE QUOTABLE RONALD REAGAN

✒ Public Service

---

*T*here are some days when you go home so frustrated that you get in the shower and make speeches to the walls. But there are other days when you go home and feel ten feet tall because you have solved a problem.

— Meet the Students, *taping for television, March 7, 1973*

✒

... *W*e should also answer the central question of public service: Why are we here? What do we believe in? Well for one thing, we're here to see that government continues to serve the people and not the other way around. Yes, government should do all that is necessary, but only that which is necessary.

— *Address accepting the Republican presidential nomination,*
Dallas, Texas, August 23, 1984

✒ Quips

___

George, here we are on the late show again.

> — *Aside to Senator (and former film song-and-dance man) George Murphy by Reagan at his first inaugural as Governor of California, 12:01 AM, January 3, 1967*

✒

You know, after you've canceled Social Security and started the war, what else is there for you to do?

> — *Remarks in response to President Jimmy Carter's charge that Reagan was out to destroy the U.S. and the world, Milwaukee, Wisconsin, October 1980*

Rapid Transit

Everybody driving on the freeway in the rush hour is looking at the traffic and saying, "We should have rapid transit because if we did, all those people would be riding and I would have the freeway to myself."

— Meet the Students, *taping for television, Sacramento, April 21, 1973*

🖋 Reagan, Nancy

Nancy, in front of all your friends here today, let me say, thank you for all you do. Thank you for your love. And thank you for just being you.

— *Remarks at a luncheon honoring Mrs. Reagan,*
New Orleans, August 15, 1988

✒ Regulation, Government

We're trying to take off the back of business a horde of unbelievable and unnecessary regulations that [government] bureaucracy over the years... has spawned. I believe in an old rule that [says] "If it ain't broke, don't fix it." And government's been trying to fix things too long that weren't broke.

— *Remarks at Control Data Institute, Pittsburgh, Pennsylvania, April 6, 1983*

✍ Religious Values

I believe with all my heart that standing up for America means standing up for the God who has so blessed our land. We need God's help to guide our nation through stormy seas. But we can't expect Him to protect America in a crisis if we just leave Him over on the shelf in our day-to-day living.

— Address to the U.S. Savings Associations, New Orleans, November 16, 1982

✍

*T*he Founding Fathers believed that faith in God was the key to our being a good people and America's becoming a great nation.

— Remarks at a White House meeting with women leaders of Christian religious organizations, October 13, 1983

THE QUOTABLE RONALD REAGAN

 Reporters

...*I* personally liked most of the men and women who covered the White House.

— From Ronald Reagan's memoir, An American Life, *1990*

❧ Retirement

When it comes to retirement, the criterion should be fitness for work, not year of birth. Our studies suggest that ending forced retirement based solely on age will have minimal consequences on the employment of other groups and will help to erase the unjust perception that persons over 70 are less productive than their fellow citizens. We know that many individuals have valuable contributions to make well beyond 70 years of age, and they should have the opportunity to do so if they desire.

— Remarks on signing the Older Americans Month proclamation,
The White House, April 2, 1982

🌿 Revolution

Revolution means democracy in today's world, not the enslavement of peoples to the corrupt and degrading horrors of totalitarianism.

— Remarks to the Cuban American National Foundation,
Miami, Florida, April 28, 1990

✒ Right and Wrong

*L*oyalty, faithfulness, commitment, courage, patriotism, the ability to distinguish between right and wrong—I hope that these values are as much a part of your life as any calculus course or social science study.

— Remarks at the presentation ceremony for the Presidential Scholars Awards, June 16, 1988

✍ Risks

---

*L*et it never be said of this generation of Americans that we became so obsessed with failure that we refused to take risks that could further the cause of peace and freedom in the world.

> — *State of the Union address, U.S. Capitol, January 27, 1987*

✒ School Choice

Millions of average parents pay their full share of taxes to support public schools while choosing to send their children to parochial or other independent schools. Doesn't fairness dictate that they should have some help in carrying a double burden?

— *Address accepting the Republican presidential nomination,*
Dallas, Texas, August 23, 1984

✍ Semiconductors (computer chips)

We're not merely accelerating the processes of the Industrial Revolution; we're fundamentally transforming it. Let me give you just one example: the semiconductor, or computer chip. One scientist makes this comparison: If automotive technology had progressed as fast as semiconductor technology in the past 20 years… a Rolls Royce would now cost less than $3, get three million miles to the gallon, deliver enough power to drive an ocean liner, and six of them would fit on the head of a pin.

— *Remarks at a question-and-answer session of the City Club of Cleveland, Ohio, January 11, 1988*

THE QUOTABLE RONALD REAGAN

*I*ts value isn't in the sand from which it is made, but in the microscopic architecture designed into it by ingenious human minds.

— Remarks to students at Moscow State University, Moscow, May 31, 1988

*"T*o see the universe in a grain of sand," is no longer a poetic metaphor, but the daily reality of the silicon chip. F. Scott Fitzgerald wrote that when the early explorers first looked on this land, they must have held their breath. They had, for the first time in history, come face-to-face with something commensurate with man's infinite capacity for wonder. Yet it was not the last time. We, too, stand on the shores of something as vast—of an economic and technological future immense with promise.

— Remarks at the annual meeting of the Atlantic Council, Washington, D.C., June 13, 1988

❧ Separation of Church and State

To those who cite the First Amendment as reason for excluding God from more and more of our institutions everyday, I say: The First Amendment of the Constitution was not written to protect the people of this country from religious values; it was written to protect religious values from government tyranny.

— *Address to the National Association of Evangelicals,*
Orlando, Florida, March 8, 1983

❧

When our Founding Fathers passed the First Amendment, they sought to protect churches from government interference. They never intended to construct a wall of hostility between government and the concept of religious belief itself.

— *Address to the National Association of Evangelicals,*
Orlando, Florida, March 8, 1983

THE QUOTABLE RONALD REAGAN

 Sermons

---

*T*alking to a church audience like this reminds me a little of a church in a little town in Illinois—Dixon, Illinois—that I used to attend as a boy. One sweltering Sunday morning in July, the minister told us he was going to preach the shortest sermon he had ever given. And then he said a single sentence: "If you think it's hot today, just wait."

— Remarks at the annual convention of the National Association of Evangelicals, Columbus, Ohio, March 6, 1984

✒ Sexually-Explicit Movies

In those days you would see a hand reach out and hang the "Do Not Disturb" sign on the door.

— Frequently mentioned by Reagan when comparing his movie days with later ones

✌ Sherman-like Statements

I never found anyone but Sherman who ever said that, so I figure it's his line.

— Response to a reporter who asked if he would flatly deny that he would allow his name to be placed in nomination for the presidency at the Republican National Convention at Miami Beach, Florida, 1968

Shining City on a Hill, A

I've spoken of the shining city all my political life, but I don't know if I ever quite communicated what I saw when I said it.... In my mind it was a tall, proud city built on rocks stronger than oceans, windswept, God-blessed, and teeming with people of all kinds living in harmony and peace; a city with free ports that hummed with commerce and creativity. And if there had to be city walls, the walls had doors and the doors were open to anyone with the will and the heart to get there. That's how I saw it, and see it still.

— *Farewell Address to the Nation, The White House, January 11, 1989*

Skepticism

…At this point in my career I'm used to a certain amount of skepticism. Back in 1966, when somebody told my old boss, Jack Warner, that I was running for Governor of California, he thought a minute and said, "No, Jimmy Stewart for governor; Reagan for best friend."

— *Remarks at a briefing for state and local officials on the Economic Bill of Rights, The White House, July 22, 1987*

❧ Soviet Union, The

*I*n an ironic sense, Karl Marx was right. We are witnessing today a great revolutionary crisis, a crisis where the demands of the economic order are conflicting directly with those of the political order. But the crisis is happening not in the… West, but in the home of Marxism-Leninism, the Soviet Union. It is the Soviet Union that runs against the tide of history by denying human freedom and human dignity to its citizens.

> — *Address to members of the British Parliament,*
> *Palace of Westminster, London, June 8, 1982*

❧

*W*hen was the last time you bought a car—even a good cheese or videocassette recorder—and the label read, "Made in the U.S.S.R."?

> — *Remarks at the annual convention of the National Association of Counties,*
> *Indianapolis, Indiana, July 13, 1987*

THE QUOTABLE RONALD REAGAN

✒ Space Exploration

We will never forget them, nor the last time we saw them, this morning, as they prepared for their journey and waved good-bye and "slipped the surly bonds of earth" to "touch the face of God."

— *Address to the nation on the Space Shuttle Challenger disaster, The Oval Office, January 28, 1986*

✒

When we come to the edge of our known world, we're standing on the shores of the infinite. Dip your hand in that limitless sea; you're touching the mystery of God's universe. Set sail across its waters and you embark on the boldest, most noble adventure of all. Out beyond our present horizons lie whole new continents of possibility, new worlds of hope, waiting to be discovered.

— *Remarks to participants in the Young Astronauts Program, June 11, 1986*

Statesmanship

The challenge of statesmanship is to have the vision to dream of a better, safer world and the courage, persistence and patience to turn that dream into a reality.

— *Remarks to the U.S. negotiating team for the Nuclear and Space Arms Negotiations with the Soviet Union, Washington, D.C., March 8, 1985*

 # Statism

Those who preach the supremacy of the state will be remembered for the sufferings their delusions caused their peoples.

— Address at the Captive Nations Week Conference, Beverly Hills, California, July 15, 1991

✒ Statue of Liberty

The poet called Miss Liberty's torch the "lamp beside the golden door." Well, that was the entrance to America, and it still is…. The glistening hope of that lamp is still ours. Every promise, every opportunity is still golden in this land. And through that golden door our children can walk into tomorrow with the knowledge that no one can be denied the promise that is America.

— Address accepting the Republican presidential nomination,
Dallas, Texas, August 23, 1984

✒

I told Nancy, "This is the other woman in my life."

— Remark to Mrs. Reagan as their helicopter circled the statue prior to his landing to give an address at the Statue of Liberty Centennial Ceremony, Governor's Island, New York, July 3, 1986

❦ Status Quo

"Status quo," you know, that is Latin for "the mess we're in."

*— Remarks at a reception for members of the
Associated General Contractors of America, The White House, March 16, 1981*

✹ Strategic Defense Initiative (SDI)

... This new defense system... is the most hopeful possibility of our time. Its primary virtue is clear. If anyone ever attacked us, [the] Strategic Defense Initiative would be there to protect us. It could conceivably save millions of lives.... SDI is arms control.

— *Remarks at the Conservative Political Action Conference,*
Washington, D.C., March 1, 1985

Strikes, Public Employee

I believe in collective bargaining in the private sector. I do not believe in it for the public sector because I do not believe that public employees can be allowed to strike. Public employees are striking against the people, and the people are the highest source of power, other than the Lord Himself, that the government has.

— Meet the Students, *taping for television, Sacramento, April 12, 1973*

✑ Students

I wish all American students were as interested in their studies as you evidently are.... And I wish all teachers and parents took an interest in their children's educational development as your parents and teachers have taken in yours.

> — *Remarks on greeting the finalists of the National Spelling Bee,*
> *The White House Rose Garden, June 6, 1983*

❦ Summit Meetings, U.S.-U.S.S.R.

*M*y mission, stated simply, is a mission for peace.

— *Address to the nation on his upcoming summit meeting with Mikhail Gorbachev in Geneva, The Oval Office, November 14, 1985*

❧ Supply and Demand, Law of

No one has yet found a way to repeal the Law of Supply and Demand.

— Remarks at the Roy Crocker dinner, Pasadena, California, November 21, 1972

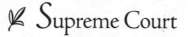# Supreme Court

The only litmus test I wanted... was the assurance of a judge's honesty and integrity.... I wanted judges who would interpret the Constitution, not try to rewrite it.

— *From Ronald Reagan's memoir,* An American Life, *1990*

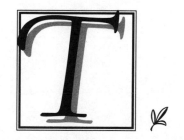

✍ Taiwan

In our relationship with China, we should always remember what our Chinese friends on Taiwan have accomplished: a resource-poor island has become one of the major trading nations of the world; a political transformation... has resulted in full-fledged democracy.

— Address at the Captive Nations Week Conference,
Beverly Hills, California, July 15, 1991

❧ Taxes

Government does not tax to get the money it needs; government always finds a need for the money it gets.

> — *Remarks at a White House luncheon for out-of-town editors and broadcasters, July 22, 1981*

❧

Flatter rates mean more reward for that extra effort.

> — *Remarks on signing the Tax Reform Act into law, The White House South Lawn, October 22, 1986*

Common sense told us that when you put a big tax on something, the people will produce less of it. So, we cut the people's tax rates, and the people produced more than ever before.

— *Farewell Address to the Nation, The White House, January 11, 1989*

✒ Tax Cuts

I've been told that some members of Congress disagree with my tax cut proposal. Well, you know it's been said that taxation is the art of plucking the feathers without killing the bird. It's time they realized the bird just doesn't have any feathers left.

— *Remarks at the Midwinter Congressional City Conference of the National League of Cities, Washington, D.C., March 2, 1981*

✒

I know you have been told by some that we should do away with the tax cuts in order to reduce the deficit. That's like trying to pull a game out in the fourth quarter by punting on third down.

— *Radio address to the nation, April 3, 1982*

$\mathcal{W}$hen John F. Kennedy's tax program... which was not too dissimilar to ours... was passed, the same thing happened—more revenues at lower [tax] rates. It happened back in Coolidge's administration, and they cut the taxes several times in that period.

— Remarks at a meeting with economic reporters,
The White House, June 16, 1987

✒ Taxpayers

Our loyalty lies with little taxpayers, not big spenders. What our critics really believe is that those in Washington know better how to spend your money than you, the people, do. But we're not going to let them do it, period.

— *President's news conference, The White House, June 30, 1982*

✒ Tax Revolts

England may be the mother of parliaments, but from the Boston Tea Party to this administration, it's the United States that has been the mother of tax revolts. You know, that's a pretty good line. I can hardly wait to try it out on Margaret Thatcher.

> — *Remarks at a briefing for members of the American Business Conference, The White House, March 23, 1988*

✒ Teachers

Teachers should be paid and promoted on the basis of their merit and competence. Hard-earned tax dollars should encourage the best. They have no business [being] rewarded for incompetence and mediocrity.

— *Address at Seton Hall University, South Orange, New Jersey, May 21, 1983*

✒ Television and Politics

*T*elevision… is actually a return to our old-time tradition of taking to the stump. When our nation was sparsely settled, it was possible for a candidate making the circuit to be seen by almost all the voters. As we grew in size and numbers, only a few actually saw the candidate. They made their decision on what they had heard or read about him.

But now, via the medium of television, they can all see him and hear him. And let me reveal something known to actors—you can't lie to the camera. When it rolls in for that bigger-than-life closeup, you'd better mean what you say, for insincerity will show up like a putty nose.

— Address to United Press International editors, San Francisco, 1969

✒ Terrorism
---

*H*ow many of our citizens can be kidnapped by a foreign power before the rest of us decide that we have reached a point at which we have to do something about it?.... I do know what the limit is in my mind. I think the limit is one.

— *Governor's news conference, Sacramento, January 30, 1968*

✒

*O*ur evidence is direct; it is precise; it is irrefutable.

— *Address to the nation on the reasons for a preemptive anti-terrorism air strike on Libya, The Oval Office, April 14, 1986*

Terrorism is the preferred weapon of weak and evil men.

— Remarks at a meeting with members of the American Business Conference,
The White House, April 15, 1986

🌿 Thatcher, Margaret

Margaret Thatcher is a remarkable lady whose achievements will be appreciated more and more as time goes on. For me, she has been a staunch ally and good friend. I salute her.

> — *Address to the Cambridge Union Society,*
> *Cambridge, England, December 5, 1990*

✍ Third-Party Movements

I don't have much faith in the third-party movement. I think a third party usually succeeds in electing the people it set out to oppose.

— *Radio interview, San Francisco, August 29, 1975*

✒ Trade Protectionism

We and our trading partners are in the same boat. If one partner shoots a hole in the boat, it makes no sense for the other partner to shoot another hole in the boat. That's not getting tough; it's getting wet. And, eventually, it means sinking the boat that's headed for greater growth and prosperity. Protectionism only opens the door to retaliation.

— *Teleconference with the U.S. Chamber of Commerce, May 10, 1983*

✒ Tragedy

Tragedy is nothing new to mankind, but somehow it is always a surprise [and] never loses its power to astonish.

— *Remarks at the memorial service for members of the Army's*
101st Airborne Division, killed in an airplane crash,
Fort Campbell, Kentucky, December 16, 1985

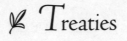 Treaties

The history of treaties throughout the centuries is such that one should not want to stake one's life on a treaty.

— *Address to the Cambridge Union Society,*
Cambridge, England, December 5, 1990

🌿 Trust (Between Nations)

... The importance of this treaty transcends numbers.
We have listened to the wisdom in an old Russian maxim.
I'm sure you are familiar with it, Mr. General Secretary [Gorbachev]....
The maxim is: *Dovorey no provery*—Trust, but verify.

— *Remarks on signing the INF treaty, the first to eliminate an entire class of nuclear weapons, The White House, December 8, 1987*

✒ Twenty-First Century

$\mathcal{M}$y hope is that in the 21st century... human dignity will be everywhere respected.

> — *Address at the Captive Nations Week Conference,*
> *Beverly Hills, California, July 15, 1991*

United Nations, The

On this U.N. anniversary, we acknowledge its successes: the decisive action during the Korean war, negotiation of the non-proliferation treaty, and the laudable achievements by the United Nations High Commissioner for Refugees. Nor must we close our eyes to this organization's disappointments; its failures to deal with real security issues, the total inversion of morality in the infamous Zionism-is-racism resolutions, the politicization of too many agencies, the misuse of too many resources. The U.N. is a political institution, and politics requires compromise. We recognize that, but let us remember from those first days, one guiding star was supposed to light our path toward the U.N. vision of peace and progress—a star of freedom.

— Address to the 40th Session of the United Nations General Assembly,
New York City, October 24, 1985

United States, Challenges to the

... *B*ecause we are a great nation, our challenges seem complex. It will always be this way. But as long as we remember our first principles and believe in ourselves, the future will always be ours.

— *Farewell Address to the Nation, The White House, January 11, 1989*

THE QUOTABLE RONALD REAGAN

✤ Unity

Today... for all who fought here, we celebrate the triumph of democracy. We reaffirm the unity of democratic peoples who fought a war and then joined with the vanquished in a firm resolve to keep the peace.

— *Remarks at the 40th anniversary of D-Day, Omaha Beach, Normandy, France, June 6, 1984*

Universities, The Role of

A university is a place where ancient tradition thrives alongside the most revolutionary of ideas. Perhaps as no other institution, a university is simultaneously committed to the day before yesterday and the day after tomorrow.

— *Address to the Oxford Union Society, Oxford, England, December 4, 1992*

✒ Unknown, Braving the

The greatest victories come when people dare to be great, when they summon their spirits to brave the unknown and go forward together to reach a greater good.

— Remarks at a meeting of Chinese community leaders,
Beijing, China, April 27, 1984

⚘ U.S. Marine Corps

They [The Marines] have given willingly of themselves so that a nearly defenseless people in a region of great strategic importance to the free world will have a chance someday to live lives free of murder and mayhem and terrorism.

— Address to the nation following a suicide bomb attack on Marine barracks in Beirut, Lebanon, killing more than 200 Marines, The Oval Office, October 27, 1983

✍ Values

An America that is militarily and economically strong is not enough. The world must see an America that is morally strong with a creed and a vision. This is what has led us to dare and achieve. For us, values count.

— Remarks at the annual convention of the
Congressional Medal of Honor Society,
New York City, December 12, 1983

✍

We've been blessed with the opportunity to stand for something— for liberty and freedom and fairness. And these are things worth fighting for, worth devoting our lives to.

— Remarks at the Conservative Political Action Conference,
Washington, D.C., March 1, 1985

✿ Veterans, Fallen in Battle

It is, in a way, an odd thing to honor those who died in defense of our country… in wars far away. The imagination plays a trick. We see these soldiers in our mind as old and wise. We see them as something like the Founding Fathers, grave and gray-haired. But most of them were boys when they died, and they gave up two lives—the one they were living and the one they would have lived. When they died, they gave up their chance to be husbands and fathers and grandfathers. They gave up their chance to be revered old men. They gave up everything for their country, for us. All we can do is remember.

— *Remarks at Veterans' Day ceremony, Arlington National Cemetery, Arlington, Virginia, November 11, 1985*

✿ Vietnam War, Lessons of

$\mathcal{P}$erhaps at this late date, we can all agree that we've learned one lesson: that young Americans must never again be sent to fight and die unless we are prepared to let them win.

— Remarks at Veterans' Day ceremony, The Vietnam Veterans' Memorial, Washington, D.C., November 11, 1988

Vision of America

Together, let us make this a new beginning. Let us make a commitment to care for the needy, to teach our children the values and the virtues handed down to us by our families, to have the courage to defend those values and the willingness to sacrifice for them.

Let us pledge to restore, in our time, the American spirit of voluntary service, of cooperation, of private and community initiative, a spirit that flows like a deep and mighty river through the history of our nation.

— Speech accepting the Republican presidential nomination,
Detroit, July 17, 1980

✒ Volunteering in Time of Need

... *Y*ou did what Americans have done for more than two centuries. When others were in need, you didn't point to the other guy. You rolled up your sleeves and went to work.

— *Honoring the residents of Chase, Maryland, for their rescue work in the wake of a major train wreck, The Old Executive Office Building, February 3, 1987*

✒ Volunteerism

Wouldn't it be better for the human spirit and for the soul of this nation to encourage people to accept more responsibility to care for one another, rather than leaving those tasks to paid bureaucrats?

— *Remarks at a luncheon for black clergymen,*
The White House, March 26, 1982

✒ War

*H*istory teaches that wars begin when governments believe the price of aggression is cheap.

— *Address to the Nation, U.S. Allies, and the Soviet Union,*
The White House, January 6, 1984

❦ Washington, George

$\mathcal{Y}$es, he is first in our hearts and will be there for all time. But as Abraham Lincoln said, "To add brightness to the sun, or glory to the name of Washington, is… impossible. Let none attempt it… pronounce the name and… leave it shining on."

— Remarks at commemoration of the 250th anniversary of Washington's birth, Mount Vernon, Virginia, February 22, 1982

❦

The image of George Washington kneeling in prayer in the snow is one of the most famous in American history. He personified a people who knew it was not enough to depend on their own courage and goodness; they must also seek help from God, their Father and Preserver.

— Christmas radio address to the nation, December 24, 1983

THE QUOTABLE RONALD REAGAN

✒ Washington, D.C., Ways of

I should warn you that things in this city aren't often the way they seem. Where but in Washington would they call the department that's in charge of everything outdoors… the Department of the Interior?

— *Remarks at the dinner of the Republican National Hispanic Assembly,*
September 14, 1983

✒

I've learned in Washington that that's the only place where sound travels faster than light.

— *Remarks at the annual convention of the Congressional Medal of Honor Society,*
New York City, December 12, 1983

Back then [before 1981], government's view of the economy could be summed up in a few short phrases: If it moves, tax it. If it keeps moving, regulate it. And if it stops moving, subsidize it.

— Remarks to state chairpersons of the National White House Conference on Small Business, August 15, 1986

⚘ Welfare

Welfare needs a purpose: to provide for the needy, of course, but more than that, to salvage these, our fellow citizens, to make them self-sustaining and, as quickly as possible, independent of welfare. There has been something terribly wrong with a program that grows ever larger even when prosperity for everyone else is increasing. We should measure welfare's success by how many people leave welfare, not by how many are added.

— *Remarks at the Governor's Conference on Medicaid, San Francisco, 1968*

*M*any people today are economically trapped in welfare. They'd like nothing better than to be out in the workaday world with the rest of us. Independence and self-sufficiency is what they want. They aren't lazy or unwilling to work; they just don't know how to free themselves from the welfare security blanket.

— Remarks to the National Alliance of Business, October 5, 1981

*T*he war on poverty created a great new upper-middle class of bureaucrats that found they had a fine career as long as they could keep enough needy people there to justify their existence.

— Remarks at a Kansas Republican Party luncheon, Topeka, September 9, 1982

THE QUOTABLE RONALD REAGAN

✍ White House, The

*W*elcome here to your house, which you're letting me live in for a while.

> — *Remarks at a reception opening the Champions of American Sport exhibition, The White House, June 22, 1981*

✿ Wisdom

... We're returning to the age-old wisdom of our culture, a wisdom contained in the book of Genesis in the Bible: In the beginning was the spirit, and it was from this spirit that the material abundance of creation issued forth.

— *Remarks to students at Moscow State University,*
Moscow, May 31, 1988

✒ Women

Our commitment to fairness means that we must assure legal and economic equity for women and eliminate, once and for all, all traces of unjust discrimination against women from the United States Code.

— *State of the Union address, U.S. Capitol, January 25, 1983*

✒

Women… are a diverse majority with varied interests and varied futures. Some seek to start their own businesses. Some seek to advance in their chosen careers. Some seek to focus on the home and the family. Some seek political office. And some women seek to do all of these things.

— *Remarks to the Republican Women's Forum, San Diego, August 26, 1983*

✦ Work

Work and family are at the center of our lives, the foundation of our dignity as a free people.

— Speech accepting the Republican presidential nomination,
Detroit, July 17, 1980

# World Trade

Constructive trade, the two-way exchange of goods and services, is the most efficient and logical way for each nation… to build a stable prosperity, a prosperity based not on aid, but on mutually beneficial economic contacts.

— *Remarks to the California International Trade Conference,*
Sacramento, May 22, 1974

*I*n dealing with our economy, more is in question than just prosperity. Ultimately, peace and freedom are at stake. The United States took the lead after World War II in creating an international trading and financial system that limited government's ability to disrupt trade. We did this because history had taught us [that] the freer the flow of trade across the borders, the greater the world economic progress and the greater the impetus for world peace.

— Remarks to the Commonwealth Club of California,
San Francisco, March 4, 1983

✌ *Youth*

...*I*t wasn't so very long ago that all I had to do to start an unfriendly campus riot was [to] show up. And now on campaign stop after campaign stop, in state after state, I've seen so many young Americans, like yourselves, coming out to say "hello."

— Remarks at a Republican campaign rally,
Mount Clements, Michigan, November 5, 1988

✌

I'm not suggesting you should close the door on youth because you are graduating from college today. Heck, I certainly haven't, and I'm old enough to be your father! Or *his* father! Or maybe even *his* father!

— Commencement address, Eureka College, Eureka, Illinois, May 9, 1992

*L*ive each day to the fullest. Live each day with enthusiasm, optimism and hope. If you do, I am convinced that your contribution to this wonderful experiment we call America will be profound.

— *Commencement address, Eureka College, Eureka, Illinois, May 9, 1992*

 Zero Defects

... *The* he institution of "zero defects" in industry—by which employees strive to avoid error in the manufacturing process—has certainly aided in the achievement of error-free products.

— Governor's proclamation, Sacramento, March 6, 1969

✌ Zest

*H*e said, "There's a rising Tide of good Cheer and Joy in the land. We see new Zest in the economy every day. And, all we need now is a bold Dash to Safeguard the gain we've made already." I said, "Thanks," and congratulated him on the Top Job that you're all doing in support of tax fairness.

— Remarks to employees of Procter & Gamble's Ivorydale soap manufacturing plant, St. Bernard, Ohio, October 3, 1985

✒ Bibliography

President Reagan's Quotations, edited by Clark Cassell. Braddock Publications, Washington, D.C., 1984.

The Quotable Ronald Reagan, edited and compiled by Joseph R. Holmes. JRH & Associates, Inc., San Diego, California, 1975.

The Reagan Wit, edited by Bill Adler with Bill Adler, Jr. Caroline House Publishers, Aurora, Illinois, 1981.

The Reagans: A Political Portrait, by Peter Hannaford. Coward-McCann, New York, 1983.

Remembering Reagan, by Peter Hannaford and Charles D. Hobbs. Regnery Publishing, Inc., Washington, D.C., 1994.

Revolution, by Martin Anderson. Harcourt Brace Jovanovich, San Diego, 1988.

Ronald Reagan: A Political Biography, by Lee Edwards. Nordland Publishing International, Houston, Texas, 1981.

Ronald Reagan Talks to America, Devin Adair Company, Old Greenwich, Connecticut, 1983.

Ronald Reagan: The Wisdom and Humor of The Great Communicator, edited by Frederick J. Ryan, Jr. Collins Publishers, San Francisco, 1995.

A Shining City: The Legacy of Ronald Reagan, edited by Erik Felten. Simon & Schuster, New York, 1998.

Speaking My Mind: Selected Speeches, by Ronald Reagan. Simon and Schuster, New York, 1989.

Speeches of Ronald Reagan, archives of the Ronald Reagan Presidential Library, Simi Valley, California; Hoover Institution, Stanford University, Palo Alto, California.